Dutch Oven COOKING

TERRY LEWIS

Photographs by ZAC WILLIAMS

GIBBS SMITH
TO ENRICH AND INSPIRE HUMANKIND

First Edition
15 14 13   6 5

Text © 2011 Terry Lewis
Photographs © 2011 Zac Williams

Published by
Gibbs Smith
P.O. Box 667
Layton, Utah 84041

1.800.835.4993 orders
www.gibbs-smith.com

Designed by Kurt Wahlner
Printed and bound in China

Gibbs Smith books are printed on either
recycled, 100% post-consumer waste, FSC-
certified papers or on paper produced from
sustainable PEFC-certified forest/controlled
wood source. Learn more at www.pefc.org.

Library of Congress Cataloging-
in-Publication Data

Lewis, Terry, 1960-
  Dutch oven cooking / Terry Lewis ;
photographs by Zac Williams. — 1st ed.
     p. cm.
  ISBN 978-1-4236-1459-3
1. Dutch oven cooking. 2. Cookbooks. I.
Title.
  TX840.D88L48 2011
  641.5'89—dc22
                                  2010045872

For the three wonderful and patient women who taught me to cook;
my mother, Carolyn Nadean Roberts Lewis, and my grandmothers,
Angeline Lunceford Lewis and Florence Wilson Roberts

And for my daughter and cooking partner, Victoria (Tori) Marie Lewis

Contents

Intermediate

Advanced

Introduction

I believe to have a success with anything; you need to start with quality equipment and ingredients. It is no different with Dutch oven cooking. I use Dutch ovens from Camp Chef and Lodge because they are the best quality, and I prefer Kingsford charcoal to use for cooking. As far as ingredients are concerned, use only high quality products for the best results.

Dutch ovens

Most Dutch ovens come seasoned and ready for use. All you have to do is wash them. Over time, with continued use, your oven will build up a better coating or season. Right after cooking is the best time to clean your oven. I wash mine with water and a little soap, but do not scrub the coating away or you will have to start over with the seasoning process. Heat the Dutch oven in your house oven or over a camp stove or coals to get it completely dry. Wipe it down with a little oil or cast iron conditioner. I use a conditioner sold by Camp Chef that I really like.

Heat

Learning to control the heat is one of the trickiest parts about cooking in Dutch ovens, but once you do, you will have great success. In this cookbook I have provided the number of coals to use for each recipe. Always place the bottom coals in a ring shape underneath the oven. The heat goes to the middle, so until you have some experience, don't put coals in the center of the ring. The top coals should be in an evenly spaced pattern around the lid of the Dutch oven. A good rule of thumb for the amount of coals needed is to use twice the number of coals as the oven is in inches—for instance, using a 12-inch oven, you need 12 coals for the top and 12 for the bottom, or 24. But you don't put them on that way; you put two-thirds of the 24 on the top, or 16, and one-third on the bottom, or 8. You may need to tweak this formula as you become practiced, but it is a good starting point. For most recipes, the baking temperature is about 350 degrees, and this formula achieves that temperature. You can raise or lower the temperature by adding or removing 1 coal for approximately every 20 degrees you need to adjust.

Tools

It is easy to spend a lot of money on tools for Dutch oven cooking. Before you go out and buy a bunch of equipment, I recommend that you find someone who cooks with Dutch ovens and ask about which tools they like. If you can attend a Dutch oven competition or gathering, you can see many different tools and how they work. This way you won't buy something that isn't going to work for you. It's like test driving cars. Below is a list of items that will get you started on your way to successful Dutch oven cooking.

- Several good quality Dutch ovens—the 12-inch is the most popular and most recipes in this book are geared for that size. It is useful to have a couple 12-inch ovens and one or two that are smaller and larger.

- Charcoal—plenty of it.

- Lid lifters—there are many kinds, so find the one that works best for you.

- Lid stands—very important for safety and cleanliness.

- Heavy gloves—to keep your hands safe.

- Tongs—for moving coals.

- Charcoal starter—to get your coals heating up and ready to use.

- Dutch oven table—this can go from reasonably priced to expensive, so find one you like. I used a heavy baking sheet on two cinder blocks until I found the one I wanted.

- Fold-up table—for your food preparation space.

- Camp stove—this is a great way for starting coals and heating water.

Favorite tip

Other than making sure to grease the oven prior to use, my favorite tip for Dutch oven cooking is on how to remove a beautiful pie from the oven. Here is how you do it:

Place double layer strips of parchment paper across the bottom of the Dutch oven, extending over the edges of the rim by a couple of inches, in an X pattern. Make your pie as directed in the recipe, and when it is time to remove the pie from the oven, find a friend to help. Each of you grab two legs of the X, and working together, carefully lift the pie out of the oven and place on a serving platter or lid of the Dutch oven. After it has cooled a bit and is stable, you can gently pull the parchment paper strips from under the pie. This works like a charm!

Beginner

Pizza Pull·A·Parts

12-inch Dutch oven
32 hot coals
10–12 servings

1 envelope (1.3 ounces) dry onion soup mix
1 cup grated Parmesan cheese
1 envelope (1.3 ounces) dry Italian dressing mix, divided
Dough for 1 loaf of bread, frozen bread, thawed, or
   2 cans (16.3 ounces each) refrigerator biscuits
12 to 15 pepperoni slices, cut into small pieces
6 ounces pizza sauce
$^1/_2$ cup butter, melted

Thoroughly grease Dutch oven and warm over 6–8 coals.

Combine soup mix, cheese, and 2 tablespoons dressing mix in a large ziplock bag. Cut dough into 1-inch pieces and drop into bag. Gently toss to coat pieces in the seasoning mixture.

In a large bowl, carefully mix dough, pepperoni, and pizza sauce together and then spoon dough mixture into the Dutch oven. Sprinkle remaining dressing mix on top of this mixture and pour butter on top of that. Cover and bake, using 8 coals underneath the oven and 16 on top, for approximately 20 minutes. Bread should be browned on the top when done.

Corn Bread

12-inch Dutch oven
24 hot coals
6–8 servings

1^{1}/$_{2}$ cups corn meal
^{1}/$_{2}$ cup flour
2 teaspoons baking powder
2 teaspoons sugar
1 teaspoon salt
^{1}/$_{2}$ teaspoon baking soda
^{1}/$_{4}$ cup butter, softened
1^{1}/$_{2}$ cups buttermilk
2 eggs

Mix together all ingredients, beating well for 30 seconds. Pour into greased Dutch oven, cover, and bake, using 8 coals underneath the oven and 16 on top, for 30–35 minutes or until corn bread is golden brown.

Variations: You may substitute bacon drippings for the butter and add crumbled cooked bacon to the batter. Chopped onions and bell peppers cooked in the butter or bacon fat make a spicy corn bread.

5·Bean Baked Beans

12-inch Dutch oven
39 hot coals
15–20 servings

1 pound ground sausage
1 pound bacon, cut into 1-inch pieces
1 onion, diced
1 cup catsup
2 tablespoons vinegar
$3/4$ cup molasses
1 teaspoon salt
$1^1/4$ cups brown sugar
2 tablespoons prepared mustard
1 can (15 ounces) kidney beans
1 can (15 ounces) pinto beans
1 can (15 ounces) black beans
1 can (15 ounces) pork and beans
1 can (15 ounces) hominy

In Dutch oven, cook sausage, bacon, and onion until onion is translucent over 12 coals. Drain off most of the drippings. Add all other ingredients to Dutch oven and combine.

Cover and bake, using 9 coals underneath the oven and 16–18 on top, for 60 minutes.

Cowpoke Beans

10-inch Dutch oven
26 hot coals
6 servings

6 strips bacon
$1/2$ medium onion, finely chopped
2 cans (14.5 ounces each) cut green beans, drained
$1/4$ teaspoon garlic powder

Fry bacon in Dutch oven over 12 coals, then remove from oven and crumble. Sauté onions in bacon drippings until translucent. Remove onions and take out all but 1 tablespoon of fat. Place beans in oven and heat for a couple of minutes. Add bacon, onions, and garlic powder and combine. Cover and bake, using 6 coals underneath the oven and 8 on top, for 12 minutes.

Variations: You may add bell peppers, chopped and cooked with onions, or top with French-fried onions and/or grated cheese of choice.

Vegetable Medley

12-inch Dutch oven
39 hot coals
12–14 servings

4 to 5 thick strips bacon
1 large onion, thinly sliced
2 cups diagonally sliced carrots
1 cup diagonally sliced celery
2 cups broccoli florets
2 cups cauliflower florets
12 to 14 new red potatoes, quartered
2 tablespoons vegetable oil
1 envelope (1.3 ounces) dry onion soup mix
1 can (10.75 ounces) cream of mushroom soup, condensed
Water

Cook bacon in Dutch oven over 12 coals, remove, and dice. Place all vegetables and oil into the Dutch oven; stir to coat. Add dry soup mix and bacon and stir. In a small bowl, combine soup with three-fourths can of water and then pour over vegetables.

Cover and bake, using 9 coals underneath the oven and 18 on top, for 40 minutes. Using a large spoon, gently turn over the vegetables once or twice while cooking, do not stir.

Variation: You may add grated cheese of choice on the top of the vegetables once they are done.

Omelet

12-inch Dutch oven
31 hot coals
8–10 servings

> 2 tablespoons butter
> 2 medium onions, chopped
> 1 cup chopped green bell pepper
> 2 cups sliced mushrooms
> 2 cups diced ham
> 12 eggs
> 1$^1/_2$ cups milk
> 1 teaspoon baking soda
> 1 cup grated cheese, of choice

Melt butter in Dutch oven over 6 coals. Cook onions, bell pepper, and mushrooms until the onions appear translucent. Add ham and cook 2 minutes.

In a large bowl, beat eggs, milk, and baking soda. Pour egg mixture over vegetables and top with cheese. Cover and bake, using 9 coals underneath the oven and 16 on top, for 20–25 minutes. Serve immediately.

Lasagna

12-inch Dutch oven
38 hot coals
12–14 servings

1^1/$_2$ pounds ground beef
Salt and pepper, to taste
4 cups pasta sauce of choice
1 package (16 ounces) wide lasagna noodles, uncooked
3 cups grated Italian blend or mozzarella cheese
16 ounces cottage or ricotta cheese
4 cups water

Brown the beef in the Dutch oven over 12 coals, drain fat, and then season with salt and pepper. Remove meat from Dutch oven and wipe the oven clean.

Starting with sauce, layer sauce, noodles, meat, and cheeses in the oven. Continue layering until ingredients are gone. End with last layer being sauce and grated cheese. Gently pour the water around the edges of Dutch oven without disturbing layers.

Cover and bake, using 9 coals underneath the oven and 17 on top, for 40–50 minutes or until noodles are tender.

Chicken and Rice

12-inch Dutch oven
38 hot coals
6–8 servings

> 1 whole chicken, cut into pieces
> Seasoning salt, to taste
> 3/4 cup vegetable oil
> 2 cups uncooked rice
> 1 can (10.75 ounces) cream of chicken soup, condensed
> 3 cups water
> 1 1/2 cups grated cheese, of choice

Remove skin from chicken pieces and season meat with seasoning salt. Heat oil in Dutch oven over 12 coals and brown chicken. Remove chicken from Dutch oven and drain oil. Place rice, soup, and water in Dutch oven and mix. Place chicken in last.

Cover and bake, using 9 coals underneath the oven and 17 on top, for 40 minutes. Uncover, sprinkle cheese over chicken and rice and cook 5 minutes more.

Dutch Oven Chicken

12-inch Dutch oven
38 hot coals
6–8 servings

> 1 whole chicken, cut into pieces
> 2 cups buttermilk
> 3/4 cup vegetable oil
> 1 cup breading, mix your own or use a prepared mix*
> 1 cup water

Clean and skin chicken pieces, place in buttermilk, and let sit 30 minutes or overnight.

Heat oil in Dutch oven over 12 coals. Dip chicken pieces in breading mixture and brown in oil. Remove chicken pieces as they are browned and drain off oil. Return to Dutch oven and add water.

Cover and bake, using 9 coals underneath the oven and 17 coals on top, for 60 minutes.

*I prefer Dixie Fry brand.

NOTE: This chicken goes great with Dutch Oven Potatoes, see page 50.

Southwest Chicken

12-inch deep Dutch oven
48 hot coals
6–8 servings

> 1 tablespoon olive oil
> 1 whole chicken
> 1 teaspoon dried oregano
> $1/2$ teaspoon cumin
> 1 lime, cut into wedges
> 1 sprig cilantro

Brush oil onto the chicken. In a small bowl, crush the oregano and mix with cumin; sprinkle over the chicken and rub in. Place the lime and cilantro into the body cavity. Twist the wing tips under the chicken and tie the drumsticks together.

Place chicken in Dutch oven breast side up. Cover and bake, using 8 coals underneath the oven and 16 on top, for $1^1/2$–2 hours, replacing the coals after 50 minutes. A meat thermometer will read 180 degrees F. when done.

Barbecue Ribs

12-inch Dutch oven
60 hot coals
10–12 servings

6 pounds country-style pork ribs (beef ribs can be
substituted)
Salt and pepper, to taste
1 bottle (28 ounces) of strong barbecue sauce*

Over 12 coals, slightly brown ribs in Dutch oven and season with
salt and pepper. Cover ribs with barbecue sauce.

Cover and bake, using 8 coals underneath the oven and 14–16 coals
on top, for $1^1/_2$–2 hours. You will need to replace the coals with
new ones after 50 minutes of cooking time. If the sauce gets too
thick during cooking, add a small amount of water to thin it.

*I prefer Bull's-Eye brand.

Dutch Oven Stew

12-inch Dutch oven
36 hot coals
8–10 servings

Vegetable oil
1 pound stew meat
2 medium onions, diced
5 potatoes, cut into bite-size pieces
4 carrots, cut into bite-size pieces
3 ribs celery, cut into bite-size pieces
3 beef bouillon cubes
3 cans (10.75 ounces each) cream of mushroom soup,
   condensed
Warm water
2 envelopes (.87 ounces each) brown gravy mix
2 tablespoons soy sauce
Salt and pepper, to taste

Heat $1/4$-inch oil in the Dutch oven over 12 coals. Brown stew meat and onions. Drain off oil. Add potatoes, carrots, and celery. Add bouillon cubes and soup plus enough warm water to cover the vegetables. Stir in gravy mix and soy sauce; add salt and pepper.

Cover and bake, using 8 coals underneath the oven and 16 on top, stirring occasionally, for $1–1^{1}/2$ hours or until the vegetables are cooked.

Pot Roast

12-inch Dutch oven
60 hot coals
8–10 servings

      2 tablespoons vegetable oil
      1 (3 to 4 pound) beef roast
      1 bay leaf
      1 teaspoon salt
      1 teaspoon coarsely ground pepper
      5 carrots, diagonally sliced
      1 large onion, sliced
      2 stalks celery, thinly sliced
      1 cup beef broth
      2 cups water, divided
      6 potatoes, peeled and quartered
      1 tablespoon cornstarch

Heat Dutch oven over 12 coals. Add oil and heat. Brown meat on all sides and then add bay leaf, salt, pepper, carrots, onion, celery, broth, and 1 cup water.

Cover and bake, using 8 coals underneath the oven and 16 on top for 60 minutes. Add potatoes, cover, replace all coals, and cook for another 60 minutes. Remove roast and vegetables to a serving platter. Mix the cornstarch with remaining water and combine with meat drippings to make gravy.

Tri-Tip Roast

12-inch Dutch oven
66 hot coals
4–6 servings

> 1 (2 pound) tri-tip roast
> 2 tablespoons beef bouillon granules
> 2 cups beef broth
> $1/2$ teaspoon celery salt
> $1^1/2$ teaspoons minced onion
> $1/2$ teaspoon garlic powder
> $1/4$ teaspoon pepper
> $1/4$ teaspoon basil
> 2 cups new baby potatoes, cut into bite-size pieces
> 1 cup baby carrots
> 1 cup button mushrooms
> 1 tablespoon corn starch
> 1 cup water

Place roast in a Dutch oven. Dissolve bouillon in broth and pour over meat. In a small bowl, mix seasonings and then rub into the roast.

Cover and bake, using 10 coals underneath the oven and 12 coals on top, for 2 hours. Replace coals after 50 minutes. Add potatoes, carrots, and mushrooms, replace the coals again, and cook for an additional 60 minutes.

Remove roast and vegetables to a serving platter. Mix the cornstarch with water and combine with meat drippings to make gravy.

Easy Cobbler

12-inch Dutch oven
24 hot coals
8–10 servings

1 yellow or white cake mix
$^1/_3$ cup butter, melted
$1^1/_4$ cups milk
3 eggs
1 can (21 ounces) pie filling, flavor of choice
Whipped topping

Follow directions on cake mix package, replacing water with milk and oil with butter. Mix cake as directed on box.

Place a circle of parchment paper in bottom of Dutch oven. Put pie filling on paper and gently spoon cake mix over filling.

Cover and bake, using 8 coals underneath the oven and 14–16 coals on top, for about 40 minutes. Test cake with a toothpick. If it comes out clean, it's done. Let cake cool about 15 minutes and then turn out onto the Dutch oven lid. Carefully peel off the paper and serve with whipped topping.

Apple Crisp

12-inch Dutch oven
24 hot coals
8–10 servings

2 tablespoons lemon juice
8 cups sliced apples
$^1/_2$ cup sugar
$1^1/_2$ cups brown sugar
1 cup flour
1 cup oatmeal
$1^1/_2$ teaspoons cinnamon
$1^1/_2$ teaspoons nutmeg
$^2/_3$ cup butter, softened

In a large bowl, sprinkle juice over apples. Sprinkle sugar over the apples, tossing to coat. Place apples in lightly greased Dutch oven. Using a medium bowl, mix brown sugar and remaining ingredients together until crumbly. Sprinkle mixture evenly over the apples.

Cover and bake, using 10 coals underneath the oven and 14 on top, for 40 minutes or until apples are cooked through. Let crisp sit 15 minutes uncovered to cool and set up.

Zucchini Brownies

12-inch Dutch oven
27 hot coals
12–14 servings

2 cups flour
1^1/$_2$ cups sugar
^{1}/$_4$ cup unsweetened cocoa
1 teaspoon salt
^{3}/$_4$ teaspoon baking soda
^{1}/$_2$ cup vegetable oil
2 teaspoons vanilla
2 cups grated zucchini
Powdered sugar

In a large bowl, mix all dry ingredients. Add remaining ingredients, except for powdered sugar, and stir to moisten. Place a disk of parchment paper covering the bottom of greased Dutch oven and spoon batter onto paper.

Cover and bake, using 9 coals underneath the oven and 16–18 on the top, for 25–30 minutes. Test brownies with a toothpick inserted in center. If it comes out clean, it's done. Flip onto a plate or Dutch oven lid and dust with powdered sugar.

Variation: You may sprinkle nuts and/or chocolate chips on batter before baking.

Zucchini Cake

12-inch Dutch oven
27 hot coals
12–14 servings

1 cup oil
1^1/$_2$ cups sugar
2 teaspoons vanilla
3 eggs
1 teaspoon salt
1 teaspoon soda
2 teaspoons cinnamon
1 teaspoon nutmeg
^{1}/$_2$ teaspoon baking powder
3 cups flour
1 cup chopped nuts
2 cups grated zucchini

In a large bowl, thoroughly combine oil, sugar, vanilla, and eggs. Add dry ingredients and mix only to moisten. Add nuts and zucchini; stir to combine.

Pour batter in well-greased Dutch oven. Cover and bake, using 9 coals underneath the oven and 16–18 on top, for 45 minutes. Test cake with a toothpick. If it comes out clean, it's done.

Variations: You may add chocolate chips to batter or even frost this cake with cream cheese frosting.

Coffee Cake

10-inch Dutch oven
17 hot coals
12–14 servings

$3/4$ cup butter
2 cups sugar
2 eggs
1 teaspoon vanilla
1 cup sour cream
2 cups flour
1 teaspoon baking powder
$1/2$ teaspoon salt
$1/2$ cup chopped nuts, of choice
$1/2$ cup brown sugar
1 teaspoon cinnamon

In a large bowl, cream together butter and sugar; add eggs one at a time, beating well. Add vanilla and sour cream. Blend in flour, baking powder, and salt. Mix batter well. Pour half of the batter into well-greased Dutch oven. Sprinkle with nuts, brown sugar, and cinnamon. Add remaining batter, cover, and bake, using 7 coals underneath the oven and 9 –10 on top, for 50 minutes.

Pumpkin·Pie Cake

12-inch Dutch oven
29 hot coals
12–14 servings

Crust

1 yellow cake mix (reserve 1 cup)
1 egg, beaten
$^1/_2$ cup butter, melted

Filling

1 can (16 ounces) pumpkin
1 cup sugar
$^1/_2$ cup milk
2 eggs, beaten
$2^1/_2$ teaspoons pumpkin pie spice

Topping

1 cup reserved cake mix
$^1/_2$ cup sugar
$^1/_4$ cup butter, softened

Vanilla ice cream
Whipped topping

In a large bowl, combine crust ingredients and then pat into the bottom of greased Dutch oven. In another large bowl, combine all filling ingredients and gently pour over the crust. Using the same bowl the crust was made in, mix topping ingredients until crumbly and sprinkle evenly over filling.

Cover and bake, using 9 coals underneath the oven and 18–20 on top, for 60 minutes. Serve out of the Dutch oven with vanilla ice cream or whipped topping.

Intermediate

Cinnamon Rolls

14-inch Dutch oven
29 hot coals
15 servings

Syrup

$1/3$ cup melted butter
$1/8$ cup sugar
$3/4$ cup brown sugar
1 teaspoon cinnamon
$1/3$ cup maple syrup

Dough

2 packages (.25 ounces each) active dry yeast
$1^1/2$ cups warm water, approximately 110–115 degrees
8 teaspoons sugar
4 tablespoons vegetable oil
2 teaspoons salt
2 eggs
4 to 5 cups flour

Filling

$1/3$ cup butter, softened
$1/4$ cup sugar
2 teaspoons cinnamon
$3/4$ cup brown sugar
$2/3$ cup maple syrup
Raisins or chocolate chips, to taste (optional)

Lightly grease Dutch oven. In a small bowl, combine the syrup ingredients and then pour into the Dutch oven. Set aside.

To make the dough; dissolve yeast in water in a large bowl and let stand 5 minutes. Add sugar, oil, salt, and eggs; stir to combine. Cover with a cloth and let rise in warm place for 15 minutes. Stir down mixture and add 4 cups flour. Stir and turn onto a floured surface. Knead for 3 minutes. If sticky, knead in additional 1/2 cup flour. Roll dough into a 10 x 15-inch rectangular shape.

Spread with butter and sprinkle filling ingredients all over dough, leaving the edges free of filling. Beginning with the wide side of the rectangle, tightly roll up dough. Seal by pinching edge of the roll to the dough. Cut roll into 15 one-inch slices and place into oven on top of the syrup. Cover and rise until double, about 35–40 minutes.

Cover and bake, using 9 coals underneath the oven and 19–20 on top, for approximately 25 minutes. Watch the rolls closely toward the end of baking time. Rolls will be lightly browned and sound hollow when done. Remove from oven immediately, allowing syrup to drain over rolls.

Honey Rolls

14-inch Dutch oven
24 hot coals
12–14 servings

3 packages (.25 ounces each) active dry yeast
2 cups warm water
$1/4$ cup honey
2 tablespoons vegetable oil
2 whole eggs
1 egg, separated
1 tablespoon salt
4 to 6 cups flour
$1/2$ teaspoon cold water

In large mixing bowl, dissolve yeast in water; let stand 5 minutes. Add honey, oil, eggs, egg yolk, salt, and approximately 4 cups of flour; beat until smooth. Add additional flour until dough is slightly past sticky. Knead on floured surface for 6–8 minutes until elastic and smooth. Cover and let rise until doubled, about 60 minutes. Punch down and shape into as many 2-inch balls as the dough will make. Place into greased and warmed Dutch oven, cover, and let rise until almost doubled, about 40 minutes. Beat egg white and water; brush over the rolls.

Cover and bake, using 8 coals underneath the oven and 16 on top, for 20–25 minutes or until rolls are lightly browned.

Dutch Oven Potatoes

12-inch Dutch oven
38 hot coals
12–14 servings

6 slices of thick-cut bacon
1 onion, diced
12 potatoes, peeled and sliced in $^1/_4$-inch thick rounds
1 can (4 ounces) diced green chiles
$^1/_2$ cup water
Salt and pepper, to taste
2 cups grated cheddar cheese

Cook bacon in preheated Dutch oven, over 8–10 coals, remove from heat and crumble. Add onion to the bacon grease and cook until translucent. Put bacon back in the oven and add the potatoes, chiles, and water; season with the salt and pepper.

Cover and bake, using 9–10 coals underneath the oven and 18 on top, for 25 minutes. Remove lid and turn potatoes over, do not stir. Add more water if needed. Cook 20–25 minutes more. Remove from heat and take coals from lid. Put cheese on potatoes and replace lid for 5 minutes to melt cheese.

Twice-Baked Potatoes

12-inch Dutch oven
50 hot coals
6 servings

6 medium baking potatoes
6 tablespoons butter, softened
3 tablespoons milk
3/4 teaspoon salt
1/2 cup sour cream
1 package (8 ounces) cream cheese, cubed
1 cup grated cheddar cheese
paprika

Pierce potatoes with a fork and place in Dutch oven. Cover and bake, using 9 coals underneath the oven and 16 on top, for 60 minutes. Cool until easily handled. Cut a thin slice from the top of each potato and carefully scoop out the inside of the potato, taking care not to break the skin.

In a large bowl, whip the potatoes, butter, milk, and salt until fluffy. Beat in the sour cream and cream cheese. Spoon mixture back into potato shells. Sprinkle with cheese and paprika.

Place potatoes back in preheated Dutch oven, cover, and bake, using 9 coals underneath the oven and 16 on top, for approximately 25 minutes. Potatoes need to be heated through and the tops golden.

Broccoli Bake

10-inch Dutch oven
20 hot coals
10–12 servings

2 packages (10 ounces each) frozen chopped broccoli, thawed
and drained
1 can (10.75 ounces) cream of chicken soup, condensed
2 teaspoons lemon juice
$1/2$ cup crushed seasoned stuffing
1 tablespoon butter, melted
$1/4$ cup grated cheese, of choice

Place broccoli in lightly greased Dutch oven. In a small bowl, mix soup and lemon juice; pour over broccoli. Combine stuffing and butter in a small bowl and then sprinkle over soup mixture.

Cover and bake, using 8 coals underneath the oven and 12 on top, for 25 minutes. Remove cover and sprinkle on the cheese. Bake another 5 minutes or until the cheese is melted.

Stuffed Bell Peppers

12-inch Dutch oven
35 hot coals
4 servings

4 large red, green, or yellow bell peppers
1 can (14.5 ounces) diced tomatoes
1 large onion, chopped
2 tablespoons butter
2 cups rice, cooked
1 can (4 ounces) sliced mushrooms, drained
1 cup diced cooked ham
1 teaspoon sugar
dash hot pepper sauce
$3/4$ cup grated cheddar cheese

Cut tops off bell peppers and remove seeds and veins. Drain tomatoes, reserving juice. In Dutch oven, sauté onion in butter until tender, over 8–10 coals. Add rice, mushrooms, ham, sugar, hot pepper sauce, and tomatoes to onions. Mix well and spoon into bell peppers.

Place in Dutch oven and pour reserved juice oven bell peppers. Cover and bake, using 8–9 coals underneath the oven and 16 on top, for 40 minutes. Remove lid and sprinkle cheese on tops of bell peppers. Replace lid and cook 5 minutes longer or until cheese is melted.

Easy Breakfast

12-inch Dutch oven
10-inch Dutch oven
62 hot coals
6–8 servings

1 pound ground sausage
$1/4$ cup butter, melted
$1/4$ cup flour
$1/2$ teaspoon onion salt
$1/2$ teaspoon salt
$1/4$ teaspoon pepper
2 cups milk
6 hard-boiled eggs, coarsely chopped
1 can (15 ounces) corn, drained
$1^1/2$ cups soft bread crumbs

Cook sausage in the 12-inch Dutch oven, using 9 coals underneath the oven and 17 coals on top, until browned. Drain off grease and remove meat from oven. To the 10-inch Dutch oven, add butter, flour, salts, and pepper, stirring to combine. Add the milk and stir until sauce thickens over 10 coals.

Wipe the 12-inch Dutch oven clean. Layer half the eggs, then all of the sausage, corn, and sauce. Sprinkle on the remaining eggs and place the bread crumbs on top.

Cover and bake, using 9 coals underneath the oven and 17 coals on top, for 25–30 minutes.

Pizza

(2) 16-inch Dutch ovens
60 hot coals
6–8 servings

1^1/$_2$ cups scalded milk
1^1/$_2$ teaspoons salt
3 tablespoons butter
^{1}/$_2$ cup warm water
2 packages (.25 ounces each) active dry yeast
3 tablespoons sugar
4 cups flour
Cornmeal
Olive oil
Pizza sauce
Toppings, of choice

In a large bowl, combine milk, salt, and butter, then cool. Mix in water, yeast, and sugar; cover for 10 minutes to activate. Add flour and combine to make soft dough. Cover and place in a warm place to rise for 60 minutes. Punch down and divide dough in half.

Sprinkle a little corn meal in lightly greased Dutch ovens. Press half of the dough over the bottom of each Dutch oven. Brush each with a thin coat of olive oil and spread dough with pizza sauce and toppings.

Cover and bake, using 8–10 coals underneath each oven and 18–20 coals on top of each, for 25–30 minutes.

Variation: You can make deep-dish pizzas by using 14-inch Dutch ovens. You will need to increase the baking time by 5–10 minutes.

Buttermilk Chicken, Biscuits, and Gravy

(2) 12-inch Dutch ovens
72 hot coals
6–8 servings

Chicken

1 (2^1/$_2$ to 3) pound broiler chicken, cut up
1 cup buttermilk
1 cup flour
1^1/$_2$ teaspoons salt
^{1}/$_2$ teaspoon black pepper
^{1}/$_2$ cup vegetable oil
^{1}/$_2$ cup water

Gravy

3 tablespoons flour
1 cup buttermilk
1^1/$_2$ cups water
Salt and pepper, to taste

Biscuits

2 cups flour
2 teaspoons baking powder
^{1}/$_2$ teaspoon baking soda
^{1}/$_2$ teaspoon salt
^{1}/$_4$ cup butter-flavored shortening
^{3}/$_4$ cup buttermilk

Place chicken in a large ziplock bag with buttermilk for at least 60 minutes or overnight. In another large ziplock bag, combine flour, salt, and pepper. Drain chicken and coat each piece in the flour mixture. Let rest 10 minutes while heating the oil in a Dutch oven over 16 coals. Brown chicken and drain. Return chicken to Dutch oven and add water. Cover and bake, using 9 coals underneath the oven and 17–18 on top, for 50 minutes. Remove chicken and drain all but $1/4$ cup drippings.

To make the gravy; stir flour in drippings and cook until bubbly over same coals used to cook chicken. Add buttermilk, water, salt, and pepper, stirring constantly until gravy comes to a boil. Cook one minute longer.

Make the biscuits while the chicken is baking. Combine dry ingredients in a large bowl. Cut in shortening until mixture looks like crumbs. Add buttermilk and toss with a fork. Gently knead dough; it will be slightly sticky. Flour your hands to ease handling. Roll out dough to $1/2$- inch thickness and cut into as many $2^1/2$-inch biscuits as the dough will make. Place in a greased Dutch oven. Cover and bake, using 9 coals underneath the oven and 20 on top, for 15 minutes or until biscuits are golden brown. Serve chicken and biscuits with the gravy.

Chicken Cordon Bleu

12-inch Dutch oven
38 hot coals
8 servings

8 boneless chicken breasts
8 thin slices ham
8 slices Swiss cheese
2 eggs, beaten
1 box (6 ounces) prepared stuffing mix, crushed
   to fine crumbs
2 to 3 cups vegetable oil
2 cans (10.75 ounces each) cream of chicken soup,
   condensed
1 cup sour cream
1 can (4 ounces) chopped chiles, optional

Remove skin from breasts and pound chicken flat between 2 sheets of wax paper. Place a slice of ham and a slice cheese on each breast. Roll up and secure with a toothpick. Roll the chicken in eggs and then in the crumbs until coated.

Heat the oil in Dutch oven over 12 coals. Brown the chicken rolls in oil, then drain. Discard the oil. Wipe Dutch oven clean and return chicken to oven. In a medium bowl, combine soup, sour cream, and chiles and then pour over chicken rolls.

Cover and bake, using 9 coals underneath the oven and 17 on top, for 40–45 minutes. Do not overcook.

Roast Chicken

12-inch Dutch Oven
12-inch deep Dutch Oven
62 hot coals
6–8 servings

Stuffing

$3/4$ cup chopped onion
$1^1/2$ cups chopped celery
1 cup butter
9 cups soft bread cubes
2 teaspoons salt
$1^1/2$ teaspoons dried sage
1 teaspoon dried thyme leaves
$1/2$ teaspoon pepper

Chicken

1 whole ($2^1/2$ to 3 pounds) chicken
4 potatoes, peeled and quartered
3 carrots, peeled and sliced

In a Dutch oven, cook onions and celery in butter, over 8–10 coals, until onions become translucent. Add remaining stuffing ingredients; mix well.

Wash the chicken and fill the cavity with stuffing just before cooking.

Place chicken in the deep Dutch oven, cover, and bake, using 9 coals underneath the oven and 17 coals on top, for $1^1/4$–$1^3/4$ hours. After 40 minutes, add potatoes and carrots. You will need to replace coals after 50 minutes.

NOTE: You may use a prepared stuffing mix.

Barbecue Chicken and Barbecue Beans

14-inch Dutch oven
12-inch Dutch oven
72 hot coals
12–15 servings

Chicken

10 pounds boneless, skinless chicken breasts
1 cup vegetable oil
1 onion, chopped
1 green bell pepper, chopped
1/2 pound bacon, cooked and crumbled
1 can (12 ounces) Coke
1 bottle (12 ounces) catsup
1 1/2 cups brown sugar

Beans

1 pound bacon
4 cans (15 ounces each) Busch Baked Beans
1 green bell pepper, chopped
1 onion, chopped
1 pack (16 ounces) Lit'l Smokies
Hot sauce, to taste

In the 14-inch Dutch oven, brown chicken in oil over 12 coals. Drain off oil. Add the onion and bell pepper and sprinkle the bacon over the top. In a large bowl, combine Coke, catsup, and brown sugar; pour over chicken. Cover and bake, using 11 coals underneath the oven and 14 coals on top, for approximately 40 minutes.

To prepare the baked beans; cook bacon until crisp using the 12-inch Dutch oven over 10–12 coals. Remove from oven, drain, and crumble. Add baked beans to the Dutch oven, cover, and bring to a boil (takes approximately 10 minutes), using 9 coals underneath the oven and 14 on top. Add bell pepper, onion, Lit'l Smokies, hot sauce, and bacon; continue simmering until vegetables are cooked, 10–15 minutes.

Chicken and Cheese Chimichangas

12-inch Dutch oven
10-inch Dutch oven
50 hot coals
12 servings

$^1/_4$ cup chopped onions
1 clove garlic, minced
1 tablespoon vegetable oil
3 cups chopped chicken
1$^1/_2$ cups grated cheddar cheese
12 Rhodes Texas-size rolls
$^1/_2$ cup salsa, divided
Vegetable oil
Sour cream, grated cheddar cheese, and salsa, optional

Using the 12-inch Dutch oven, sauté onions and garlic in 1 tablespoon of oil over 10 coals. Add chicken, cover, and bake, using 9 coals underneath the oven and 17 on top, for 40 minutes. Remove from heat and sprinkle with cheese.

Flatten each roll into a 5-inch square. Spread each square with 2 teaspoons of salsa. Place $^1/_4$ cup chicken mixture on half of each square. Fold over the other half and pinch the edges to seal.

Pour oil 2–3 inches deep in the 10-inch Dutch oven and heat to about 375 degrees over 14 coals. Fry each chimichanga approximately 3 minutes on each side or until golden brown. Serve with sour cream, cheese, and salsa.

Garlic Chicken

12-inch Dutch oven
33 hot coals
2 servings

2 boneless, skinless chicken breasts
1 garlic clove, minced
2 tablespoons butter
1 medium onion, sliced
2 whole cloves
1 bay leaf
$1/4$ teaspoon salt
$1/2$ teaspoon pepper
1 cup white wine or chicken broth
1 cup sour cream

Rinse chicken with cold water and pat dry with paper towels.

Heat Dutch oven, over 12 coals, and lightly brown garlic in butter for about 2 minutes.

Add chicken and cook about 10 minutes, or until brown on all sides, turning once. Place onion on bottom of oven under chicken; add cloves and bay leaf. Sprinkle chicken with salt and pepper. In a small bowl, combine wine and sour cream and then pour over chicken. Cover and bake, using 7 coals underneath the oven and 14 on top, for 30 minutes.

Barbecue Country Pork Ribs

12-inch Dutch oven
72 hot coals
14–16 servings

> 10 pounds boneless country-style pork ribs
> 1 cup pork rub
> 1 onion, chopped
> Ginger ale
> 2 cups barbecue sauce

Cover meat with pork rub and let set 1 hour or overnight. Place meat in Dutch oven and add onion. Add enough ginger ale to cover ribs. Cover and bake, using 8 coals underneath the oven and 16 on top, for $1^1/_2$–2 hours. You will need to replace the coals after 50 minutes. After ribs are cooked, drain drippings, add barbecue sauce, cover, and bake, using 8 coals underneath the oven and 16 on top, for 30 minutes more.

Pot Roast and Vegetables

12-inch Dutch oven
84 hot coals
8–10 servings

$1/2$ cup vegetable oil
1 (4 to 5 pound) roast
1 can (14 ounces) beef broth
2 cups baby carrots
1 cup sliced mushrooms
6 potatoes, cut into 1-inch chunks
2 to 4 onions, chopped

In Dutch oven, heat oil over 12 coals. Brown roast on all sides and drain off oil. Pour broth over roast, cover, and bake, using 8 coals underneath the oven and 16 on top, for $1^1/2$ hours. Replace coals after 50 minutes.

Add all vegetables, cover and bake, using 8 coals underneath the oven and 16 on top, for another 45 minutes, stirring occasionally.

Variation: You may add other vegetables, to taste.

Fresh Berry Tart

12-inch Dutch oven
29 hot coals
6 servings

Crust

2 cups flour
1^1/$_2$ teaspoons salt
1 cup shortening
3 tablespoons cold butter
5 to 7 tablespoons water

Filling

2 cups raspberries
2 cups strawberries
2 cups blueberries
1^1/$_2$ teaspoons grated orange zest
1 teaspoon grated lemon zest
^{1}/$_4$ cup brown sugar
1 teaspoon vanilla extract

Topping

1 egg, beaten
^{1}/$_4$ cup sliced almonds

Line Dutch oven with parchment paper so that the sides of the paper extend well above the top of the oven. This will help in removing the tart from the oven to serve. See hint on page 10.

To make the crust; combine flour and salt in a medium bowl and then cut in shortening and butter until crumbs are pea-size. Add 5 tablespoons water and gently work into the crumbs to form dough. You may need a little more water. Do not over work dough after adding the water. Roll dough out to $^1/4$-inch thickness then place in Dutch oven. Once the crust is in the Dutch oven, trim excess so that sides are about 4 inches tall.

Place all filling ingredients in a large bowl and toss to coat. Spoon filling into the crust. Gently fold the crust over the filling, pleating the edges so that the filling is completely covered. Brush exposed crust with the egg and sprinkle with almonds.

Cover and bake, using 9 coals underneath the oven and 20 on top, for 40–45 minutes until the crust is browned. Cool 5 minutes in uncovered Dutch oven, remove, and serve.

Terry's Dutch Oven Brownies

12-inch Dutch oven
25 hot coals
12–14 servings

$^1/_2$ cup butter
$^1/_2$ cup margarine
$^1/_2$ cup unsweetened cocoa
2 cups sugar
4 eggs
1 teaspoon vanilla
$^1/_2$ teaspoon salt
$^1/_2$ teaspoon baking powder
$2^1/_4$ cups flour
1 cup chopped walnuts or pecans
1 package (12 ounces) chocolate chips

Melt butter and margarine in Dutch oven, over 6 coals. Pour into a large bowl, add cocoa and sugar; mix well. Add eggs, one at a time, mixing well in between additions. Stir in vanilla. In a medium bowl, combine salt, baking powder, and flour. Add to the cocoa mixture, blending only until combined. Batter will be thick. Place a circle cut from parchment paper that is the same size as the bottom of Dutch oven into the oven. Spoon batter onto paper and gently spread to cover bottom. Sprinkle nuts and chocolate chips over top of batter.

Cover and bake, using 8 coals underneath the oven and 17 on top, for 25–30 minutes. You can serve from the Dutch oven or gently turn out on a pizza pan, then turn right-side up on a platter or a cool Dutch oven lid.

Oatmeal-Chocolate Chip Cake

12-inch Dutch oven
23 hot coals
12 servings

> 1 cup oatmeal, uncooked
> 1 3/4 cups boiling water
> 1/2 cup butter, softened
> 1 cup brown sugar
> 1 cup sugar
> 3 eggs
> 1 3/4 cups flour
> 1/4 teaspoon salt
> 1 teaspoon baking soda
> 1 teaspoon unsweetened cocoa
> 1 bag (12 ounces) chocolate chips, divided*
> 3/4 cup chopped walnuts or chopped pecans

Grease Dutch oven and set aside. Place oatmeal in a large bowl and add hot water. Allow to set 10 minutes. Add butter and sugars. Mix until butter melts and all is combined. Add eggs, one at a time, mixing well in between additions.

In a medium bowl, sift flour, salt, baking soda, and cocoa together. Add flour mixture to oatmeal mixture. Stir to combine. Stir in half of the chocolate chips. Pour batter into Dutch oven. Sprinkle the top of the cake with remaining chocolate chips and nuts.

Cover and bake, using 8 coals underneath the oven and 15 coals on top, for about 40 minutes.

*I prefer semisweet but you can use milk chocolate, or even mix chocolate and butterscotch chips.

German Chocolate Cake

(3) 10-inch Dutch ovens
48 hot coals
12–14 servings

Cake

$1^3/_4$ cups flour
2 cups sugar
$^3/_4$ cup unsweetened cocoa
$1^1/_2$ teaspoons baking soda
$1^1/_2$ teaspoons baking powder
1 teaspoon salt
2 eggs
1 cup milk
$^1/_2$ cup melted butter
1 teaspoon vanilla
1 cup boiling water

German Chocolate Frosting

1 cup evaporated milk
1 cup sugar
3 egg yolks
$^1/_2$ cup butter
1 teaspoon vanilla
$1^3/_4$ cups shredded coconut
1 cup chopped roasted pecans

Chocolate Buttercream Frosting

$1/2$ cup butter, melted
$2/3$ cup unsweetened cocoa
3 cups powdered sugar
$1/3$ cup whipping cream
1 teaspoon vanilla

To make the cake; prepare two Dutch ovens by greasing sides and bottoms and placing a parchment paper disk in the bottom of each oven.

In large bowl, mix flour, sugar, cocoa, baking soda, baking powder, and salt. In another large bowl, combine eggs, milk, butter, and vanilla. Beat well with a whisk. Slowly add water into egg mixture, stirring to combine. Mix wet and dry mixtures until smooth. Evenly divide batter between Dutch ovens. Cover and bake, using 7 coals underneath each oven and 14 on top of each oven. Check if done after 30 minutes by sticking a toothpick in the center of a cake. If it comes out clean, it's done. They may need a few more minutes. Cool cakes in Dutch ovens for 10 minutes then turn out on cooling racks.

To make the German Chocolate Frosting; heat milk, sugar, egg yolks, butter, and vanilla in 10-inch Dutch oven over 6 coals and cook for 15 minutes, stirring constantly. Remove from heat and add coconut and pecans. Allow frosting to cool before using on a cool cake.

To make the Chocolate Buttercream Frosting; combine butter and cocoa, mixing well. Alternately add sugar and cream, stirring after each addition. Add vanilla and beat well. You may need to add more cream or sugar to get a good spreading consistency.

To assemble the cake; place the German Chocolate Frosting between the layers and on the top of the cake. Use the Chocolate Buttercream Frosting on the sides.

Chocolate-Topped Coffee Cake

6-inch Dutch oven
12-inch Dutch oven
31 hot coals
12–14 servings

Cake

1 cup butter, softened
2 cups sugar
2 eggs
2 cups flour
$1^1/_2$ teaspoons baking powder
$^1/_2$ teaspoon salt
1 cup sour cream
$^1/_2$ teaspoon vanilla extract

Topping

1 cup chopped pecans
2 tablespoons brown sugar
1 teaspoon cinnamon

Glaze

$^1/_2$ cup butter
$^1/_2$ cup semisweet chocolate chips

For the cake; cream butter and sugar until fluffy in a large bowl. Beat in eggs until smooth. Using another large bowl, mix dry ingredients and combine with butter mixture. Gently fold in sour cream and vanilla.

Make the topping by combining all ingredients in a small bowl.

To make the glaze; melt butter and chocolate chips in 6-inch Dutch oven over 6 coals.

Sprinkle 2 tablespoons topping into bottom of greased 12-inch Dutch oven. Pour in half of the cake batter and sprinkle with 2 more tablespoons topping. Drizzle this layer with half of the glaze. Add the remaining batter and sprinkle with the rest of the topping. Reserve remaining glaze.

Cover and bake, using 9 coals underneath the oven and 16 on top, for $1^1/4$ hours or until a toothpick inserted in center of cake comes out clean. Cool in Dutch oven 10 minutes, and then remove to serving platter. Drizzle remaining glaze over cake.

Advanced

Sourdough Herb Rolls

14-inch Dutch oven
26 hot coals
12–14 servings

2 tablespoons yeast
$^1/_3$ cup sugar
$1^1/_2$ cups warm water, divided
5 to 6 cups flour, divided
$^2/_3$ cup powdered milk
2 teaspoons salt
2 eggs, at room temperature
1 cup sourdough starter
$^1/_3$ cup vegetable oil
2 tablespoons chopped onion
$^1/_4$ cup potato flakes
1 teaspoon rosemary
$^1/_2$ cup melted butter
$^1/_2$ cup grated Parmesan cheese
$^1/_4$ cup sliced green onions

Combine yeast, sugar, and $^1/_2$ cup water. Stir to dissolve, cover, and let activate, for about 10 minutes. In a large bowl, mix 2 cups flour, milk, and salt. Then add remaining water, eggs, sourdough starter, oil, onion, potato, rosemary, and yeast mixture; thoroughly combine. Cover and let activate for about 10 minutes. Mix in enough of remaining flour to make soft, firm dough. Knead dough well, cover, and let rise to double, about 60 minutes.

Punch down and make into balls the size of a large egg. Dip each roll in melted butter then cheese and green onions. Place in greased Dutch oven so they almost touch, cheese side up. Cover and let rise, for about 30 minutes. Cover and bake, using 9 coals underneath the oven and 17 on top, for 20–25 minutes top until golden brown.

South Fork Surprise Bread

12-inch Dutch oven
24 hot coals
12–14 servings

2 packages (.25 ounces each) fast acting yeast
1 cup water
1 teaspoon honey
3^1/$_2$ cups flour
^{3}/$_4$ cup sugar
1 egg
1 tablespoon JB's premium rub
1 package (18 ounces) cream cheese, softened
^{1}/$_2$ cup diced green onions, divided
1 cup grated Colby Jack cheese
^{1}/$_4$ pound Canadian bacon, sliced
^{1}/$_2$ cup grated Parmesan cheese
^{1}/$_4$ cup butter

Put yeast in a medium bowl with water and honey. Stir to dissolve, cover, and let activate, for about 10 minutes. Place flour and sugar in a large bowl and add yeast mixture; add egg and mix well. Let rise, for about 60 minutes, punch down, and let rise again, for about 30 minutes.

Mix JB's premium rub with cream cheese and half the green onions; set aside.

Roll out dough into a 10 x 15-inch rectangle and spread cream cheese mixture onto dough. Evenly sprinkle Colby Jack on the cream cheese and then place the Canadian bacon on top of the cheese. Sprinkle remaining green onion on top and roll up dough, starting with the widest side.

Cut dough roll in half, twist each half, and place both gently in greased Dutch oven with parchment on bottom, forming a ring. Sprinkle with Parmesan cheese. Cover and bake, using 10 coals underneath the oven and 14 on top, for 25–30 minutes until golden brown and cheese is crisp. Melt butter on top and garnish as desired.

The recipe is courtesy of Damon Faust.

Awesome White Rolls

12-inch Dutch oven
24 hot coals
12 servings

2 tablespoons active dry yeast
2^1/$_2$ cups warm water, divided
^{1}/$_3$ cup sugar
^{1}/$_3$ cup vegetable oil
1^1/$_2$ teaspoons salt
1 egg
^{1}/$_3$ cup potato flakes
5 to 6 cups flour, divided
^{2}/$_3$ cup powdered milk
^{1}/$_4$ cup melted butter

In a medium bowl, combine yeast, ^{1}/$_2$ cup water, and sugar. Stir to dissolve, cover, and let activate, for about 10 minutes. Add oil, salt, egg, remaining water, and potato flakes.

In large bowl, mix 2 cups flour and milk. Then add liquid mixture, combine, cover, and let activate, for 20 minutes. Add remaining flour to make soft, firm dough. Knead well, cover, and let rise to double, for about 60 minutes.

Punch down dough and make balls the size of a large egg. Dip in butter and place in lightly greased Dutch oven. Cover and let rise again, for about 30 minutes.

Bake, using 8 coals underneath the oven and 16 on top, for 20–25 minutes until golden brown.

Stuffed Chicken-Tarragon-Cheese Rolls

12–inch Dutch oven
10-inch Dutch oven
48 hot coals
12–14 servings

Bread

1 tablespoon active dry yeast
$1^1/2$ cups warm water
$1/3$ cup sugar
5 to 6 cups bread flour, divided
$2/3$ cup powdered milk
2 teaspoons vital wheat gluten
2 eggs, at room temperature
$1/2$ cup melted butter
1 teaspoon salt

Topping

3 tablespoons dried tarragon leaves
$1/2$ cup melted butter
$1/2$ cup grated Parmesan cheese

Filling

2 large chicken breasts
1 cup chicken broth
1 package (8 ounces) cream cheese
1 can (4 ounces) green chiles, drained and finely chopped
3 tablespoons lemon juice
Salt and pepper, to taste

To make the bread; mix yeast, water, and sugar in a small bowl. Cover and let sit 10 minutes. In a large bowl, combine 2 cups flour, milk, and gluten. Add eggs, butter, and yeast mixture; stir to combine. Add salt and enough of the remaining flour to make soft dough. Place dough in a clean, greased, and warm 12-inch Dutch oven to rise to double, for about 60 minutes.

For the topping; combine tarragon and melted butter and then set aside. Place cheese in a small bowl and set aside as well.

To prepare the filling; place chicken and broth in the 10-inch Dutch oven, cover, and bake, using 7 coals underneath the oven and 14 on top, for 45 minutes. Remove chicken from Dutch oven and cool. When cool, shred with a fork. Mix in cream cheese, chiles, lemon juice, and seasonings.

When dough has doubled, punch down, and divide into 12–14 two-inch balls. Flatten each ball into $1/4$-inch thick circles. Place a rounded tablespoon of filling in center of circles. Fold dough around filling and seal. Dip rolls in topping and return to greased and warmed 12-inch Dutch oven. Cover and let rise, for about 30 minutes.

Bake, using 8–9 coals underneath the oven and 16–18 coals top, for 35–45 minutes. About 10 minutes before rolls are done, sprinkle with Parmesan cheese and return lid to finish cooking.

Stuffed Chicken Breasts

14-inch Dutch oven
10-inch Dutch oven
48 hot coals
6 servings

$^1/_4$ cup chopped onion
$4^1/_2$ teaspoons plus $^1/_4$ cup butter, divided
1 garlic clove, minced
1 package (10 ounces) frozen chopped spinach, thawed and
    squeezed dry
6 ounces cream cheese, cubed
$^1/_4$ cup seasoned bread crumbs
6 (6 ounces each) boneless, skinless chicken breast halves
$^1/_2$ teaspoon salt
$^1/_2$ teaspoon pepper
$^1/_2$ cup honey
2 tablespoons whole grain mustard
1 tablespoon lemon juice

In 14-inch Dutch oven, sauté onion in $4^1/_2$ teaspoons butter until
tender over 10 coals. Add garlic; sauté 1 minute longer. Add spinach
and cream cheese; cook and stir over low heat until blended. Remove
from heat. Stir in bread crumbs.

Flatten chicken to $^1/_4$-inch thickness; sprinkle both sides with salt
and pepper. Place about $^3/_4$ cup spinach mixture down the center of
each chicken breast half. Fold chicken over filling and secure with
toothpicks. Place in Dutch oven seam side down.

Melt remaining butter in 10-inch Dutch oven over 6–8 coals; stir in the
honey, mustard, and lemon juice. Pour over chicken. Cover and bake,
using 9–10 coals underneath the oven and 18–20 on top, for 40–45
minutes or until a meat thermometer reads 170 degrees, basting every
15 minutes with pan juices. Discard toothpicks before serving.

Sweet and Sour Meat Balls

14-inch Dutch oven
10-inch Dutch oven
40 hot coals
6 servings

Meatballs

2 pounds lean ground beef
$1/4$ cup milk
1 cup rolled oats
1 teaspoon salt
2 eggs, slightly beaten
$1/2$ teaspoon pepper
$1/2$ cup finely chopped onion
1 teaspoon Worcestershire Sauce

Sauce

$1/2$ cup brown sugar
$1/2$ cup barbecue sauce
$1/4$ cup cider vinegar
1 teaspoon Worcestershire Sauce
1 teaspoon prepared mustard

Combine meatball ingredients, mixing well. Form into meatballs about $1^1/2$ inch in diameter. Place meatballs closely together in 14-inch Dutch oven.

Mix all sauce ingredients in 10-inch Dutch oven and heat until combined over 12 coals. Pour sauce over meatballs.

Cover and bake, using 12 coals underneath the oven and 16 on top, for 30 minutes or until cooked through.

Spicy-Glazed Pork Tenderloins

12-inch Dutch oven
12 hot coals
4–6 servings

$^1/_2$ cup pineapple juice
2 limes, juiced
$^1/_2$ cup dark brown sugar
1 teaspoon ground cumin
$^1/_2$ teaspoon cayenne pepper
1 jalapeño pepper, seeded and minced
2 (12–16 ounces each) pork tenderloins
Salt and pepper, to taste
2 teaspoons vegetable oil

Stir pineapple juice, lime juice, brown sugar, cumin, cayenne, and jalapeño in small bowl. Pat tenderloins dry with paper towels and season with salt and pepper

Heat oil in Dutch oven, using 12 coals underneath the oven, until just smoking. Cook tenderloins, turning until browned on all sides, 5–8 minutes total. Reduce heat to medium by removing 3–4 coals, add lime juice mixture, and cook, rolling tenderloins to coat, until mixture is thick and syrupy and internal temperature of tenderloins registers 140 degrees, about 9–11 minutes.

Remove from heat and let meat rest under foil tent until temperature rises to 150 degrees internal temperature, about 10 minutes. Place on inverted Dutch oven lid. Spoon remaining sauce over pork. Garnish as desired.

Maple-Barbecue Baby Back Ribs with Buttered Almond Rice

(2) 10-inch Dutch ovens
(2) 12-inch Dutch ovens
134 hot coals
10 servings

Ribs

2 racks baby back ribs
1 cup pork rub
2 oranges, sliced
2 bottles (12 ounces each) lager beer

Sauce

8 slices bacon
6 cloves garlic, minced
1 small onion, finely chopped
3 jalapeños, seeded and finely chopped
1 bottle (12 ounces) lager beer
$^1/_2$ cup maple syrup or $^3/_8$ cup maple syrup
   and $^1/_8$ cup molasses
1 cup orange marmalade
1 cup catsup
1 small can tomato paste
$^3/_4$ teaspoon cayenne pepper
$1^1/_4$ teaspoons dry mustard
2 teaspoons hot sauce
2 tablespoons Worcestershire sauce
$^3/_4$ teaspoon liquid smoke
1 tablespoon vinegar

Rice

    2 tablespoons butter
    1 1/2 cups white rice
    1/3 cup slivered almonds
    3/4 teaspoon salt
    3 cups chicken stock
    1 handful flat leaf parsley, finely chopped

Remove membrane from the back of both racks of ribs. Cut between bones to separate. Coat all sides of ribs with rub and place in ziplock bags. Put sealed bags in cooler to marinate 60 minutes or overnight if time allows.

To prepare sauce; cut bacon in small chunks, cook in 10-inch Dutch oven over 7–9 coals until almost cooked. Add garlic, onion, and jalapeños. Continue to cook, stirring occasionally until onions are tender. Add beer and stir to loosen all bits stuck to the bottom of the oven. Bring to a boil over 12 coals, reduce to a medium heat by removing 4 coals, and continue to cook until reduced to half, about 20 minutes. Add all other sauce ingredients and return to a boil by adding 4–6 coals. Reduce again and simmer for 15 minutes, stirring occasionally.

After ribs have marinated, place in 12-inch Dutch oven. Put orange slices on meat. Add beer to cover ribs. Cover and bake, using 9 coals underneath the oven and 16 on top, for 1 1/2 hours, replacing coals after 50 minutes. When ribs are done, dip each rib in sauce and place in another 12-inch Dutch oven. Cover and bake, using 9 coals underneath the oven and 16 on top, for 30 minutes.

Start rice 45 minutes before you need to serve it. Melt butter in 10-inch Dutch oven over 8 coals. Add rice and almonds to oven and toast 2–3 minutes, watch this process carefully because it will burn. Add salt and stock to the oven, cover and bake, using 8 coals underneath the oven and 16 on top, for about 20 minutes or until liquid is absorbed. Remove from heat; add the parsley and fluff with fork. Serve on a large inverted Dutch oven lid. Rice on bottom, ribs arranged on rice, and sauce in a tiny Dutch oven or a hollowed out bell pepper.

Savory Rib-eye with Stuffed Mushrooms

12-inch Dutch oven
12-inch deep Dutch oven
104 hot coals
10–12 servings

Meat

1 (5–7 pound) rib-eye roast
4 cloves garlic, sliced
3 tablespoons olive oil
Canadian Steak Seasoning (Tones), to taste
$1/2$ medium onion, chopped
1 cup beef broth

Stuffed Mushrooms

$1/2$ pound Italian sausage
10 large mushrooms
$1/2$ cup chopped onion
2 cloves garlic, minced
$1/2$ pound frozen chopped spinach, thawed and drained
3 tablespoons grated Parmesan cheese
$1/2$ cup bread crumbs
6 celery stalks

Gravy

2 tablespoons cornstarch
1 cup water

To prepare the meat; preheat a 12-inch Dutch oven to about 400 degrees, using 15 coals underneath the oven and 25 on top. Make small cuts in meat and insert garlic slices. Using oil, coat all sides of meat. Press seasoning into all surfaces of beef. Place roast in hot Dutch oven and sear all sides. Remove to deep Dutch oven and cover with the onion. Add broth, carefully pouring around meat at the bottom of the oven. Cover and bake, using 9–10 coals underneath the oven and 15–17 coals on top, cooking 20 minutes per pound until internal temperature reaches 145 degrees. Coals will need to be replaced after 50 minutes.

To make the stuffed mushrooms; brown sausage in same 12-inch Dutch oven used to sear meat over 8–10 coals. Drain, reserving 1 tablespoon drippings, and return sausage and drippings to oven. Chop mushroom stems, reserving mushroom tops, and add to the sausage with onion and garlic. Cook for 3–4 minutes, stirring constantly. Remove sausage mixture to a large bowl and add spinach, cheese, and bread crumbs. Mix well and spoon mixture into mushroom tops, refrigerating until ready to cook.

You need to add mushrooms to Dutch oven about 40 minutes before meat is expected to be done. When ready to cook mushrooms, place celery stalks in bottom of Dutch oven, working around the meat, and arrange mushrooms on them. Replace lid and bake with the same coals listed above for the meat.

When meat has finished cooking, remove to a bed of lettuce. Place mushrooms around roast. To make the gravy, mix cornstarch with water and pour into hot drippings, stirring continuously until thickened. Serve the gravy in a hollowed out bell pepper.

Spinach-Stuffed Beef Tenderloin

12-inch Dutch oven
12-inch Dutch oven, with rack
58 hot coals
8 servings

1/2 pound fresh mushrooms, chopped
4 green onions, sliced
2 tablespoons olive oil, divided
2 garlic cloves, minced, divided
2 packages (16 ounces each) fresh spinach leaves
1 teaspoon salt, divided
1/8 to 1/4 teaspoon cayenne pepper
1 (3.5 pound) whole beef tenderloin, trimmed
1/4 teaspoon onion powder
1/4 teaspoon coarsely ground pepper

In 12-inch Dutch oven, sauté mushrooms and onions in 1 tablespoon oil for 2 minutes over 8–10 coals. Add half of the garlic; cook until mushrooms are tender. Add spinach, 1/2 teaspoon salt, and cayenne pepper. Cook until the spinach is wilted. Remove from the heat; set aside

Cut lengthwise slit down the center of tenderloin to within 3/4-inch of bottom. Open so meat lies flat. Spread with spinach stuffing. Fold one side of meat over stuffing; tie several times with kitchen string. Rub remaining oil over beef.

Combine the onion powder, pepper, remaining garlic, and remaining salt; rub over beef. Place on rack in Dutch oven. Cover and bake, using 8 coals underneath the oven and 16 on top, for 1–1 1/2 hours, depending on desired doneness. Replace coals after 50 minutes.

Harvest Peach-Raspberry Pie

10-inch Dutch oven
30 hot coals
8 servings

Crust

(make 2 separate recipes for this pie)
2 cups flour
1 teaspoon salt
2 tablespoons butter
$2/3$ cup shortening
5 to 8 tablespoons water

Filling

$1^{1}/3$ cups sugar
6 tablespoons clear jel
2 packages (16 ounces each) frozen peaches, thawed
1 package (16 ounces) frozen raspberries, thawed
1 teaspoon almond extract
$1/2$ teaspoon vanilla
$1^{1}/2$ teaspoons lemon juice
$1^{1}/2$ tablespoons butter, cubed
1 egg, beaten
Coarse sugar

See page 10 for tips on removing pie from Dutch oven before starting the recipe.

To make the crust; cut dry ingredients into butter and shortening until crumbs are the size of peas. Add water, combining until dough forms. Work as little as possible once you add water. Wrap in plastic wrap and chill.

For the filling; mix sugar and clear jel together in a large bowl. Add peaches, raspberries, almond extract, vanilla, and lemon juice. Gently mix together, trying not to crush berries. Set aside.

Roll out one crust recipe to $1/4$-inch thick. Place in Dutch oven to cover bottom and two-thirds way up the sides. Spoon in and level the filling. Scatter butter over the filling. Roll out remaining crust, place on pie, and seal edges with water. Using a knife, cut a couple of slits to let steam escape. Brush top with egg, and sprinkle with coarse sugar. Or, you can make a lattice top if you prefer. Cover and bake, using 12 coals underneath the oven and 18 coals on top, for 20 minutes, then reduce to 8–10 coals underneath the oven and 16 on top until crust is golden brown and filling bubbles, approximately 30 minutes.

Spiced Apple-Pear Pie

(2) 10-inch Dutch ovens
42 hot coals
8 servings

Crust

(make 2 separate recipes for this pie)
2 cups flour
1 teaspoon salt
2 tablespoons butter
$2/3$ cup shortening
5 to 8 tablespoons water

Filling

$1/2$ lemon
5 to 6 baking apples
2 to 3 pears
$1/4$ teaspoon almond extract
$2/3$ cup sugar
$1/4$ teaspoon ground cinnamon
$1/4$ teaspoon ground ginger
Generous pinch of nutmeg
$1/4$ teaspoon salt
$1/4$ cup butter
$1/4$ cup flour
$1/2$ teaspoon vanilla
1 large egg, beaten
Coarse sugar

See page 10 for tips on removing pie from Dutch oven before starting the recipe.

To make the crust; cut dry ingredients into butter and shortening until crumbs are the size of peas. Add water, combining until dough forms. Work as little as possible once you add water. Wrap in plastic wrap and chill.

For the filling; using a small bowl, finely grate the zest from the lemon; set aside. Peel, core, and slice the apples and pears and place in a large bowl. Squeeze the juice from the lemon over the fruit, add the almond extract, and toss to coat. In a small bowl, combine the sugar, cinnamon, ginger, nutmeg, and salt. Sprinkle over the fruit and stir to coat.

Melt butter in Dutch oven, using 12 coals underneath the oven. Add fruit and cook, stirring until sugar dissolves and juices simmer. Reduce heat by removing 4 coals and cook for 10 minutes until fruit softens and juices reduce some. Sprinkle in the flour, stir, and cook 2 minutes more to thicken juices. Stir in the vanilla and lemon zest.

Roll out one crust recipe to 1/4-inch thick. Place in other Dutch oven to cover bottom and two-thirds way up the sides. Spoon in and level the filling. Roll out remaining crust, place on pie, and seal edges with water. Using a knife, cut a couple of slits to let steam escape. Brush top with egg, and sprinkle with coarse sugar. Or, you can make a lattice top if you prefer. Cover and bake, using 12 coals underneath the oven and 18 coals on top, for 15–20 minutes, then reduce heat by removing 4 coals from underneath the oven and 4 from the top. Continue baking until crust is golden brown and filling bubbles, approximately 30 minutes.

Huckleberry·Apple Pie

10-inch Dutch oven
25 hot coals
8 servings

Crust

    5 cups flour
    1 tablespoon sugar
    2 cups lard
    2 teaspoons salt
    1 tablespoon vinegar
    1 teaspoon baking powder
    1 egg, beaten
    3/4 cup lukewarm water

Filling

    5 to 6 medium baking apples, cored, pared, and thinly sliced
    2 cups huckleberries
    1 egg white, lightly beaten
    1 teaspoon cinnamon
    3/4 cup of sugar
    2 teaspoons lemon juice
    1 tablespoon vanilla
    3 tablespoons cornstarch

See page 10 for tips on removing pie from Dutch oven before starting the recipe.

To make the crust; blend flour, sugar, lard, salt, vinegar, and baking powder in a large bowl. Add egg and water. Mix with a fork and then gently knead dough for a few seconds. Divide into two parts. Roll half of dough into circle that is $1/4$-inch thick. Place dough in oven and lightly push against the bottom and sides. Let the extra dough hang over the top edge of the Dutch oven.

For the filling; place apples and huckleberries in a large bowl. Using as small bowl, mix the remaining ingredients and then pour over the fruit. Lightly stir until evenly coated. Pour filling into the pastry-lined Dutch oven, spreading out evenly.

Roll remaining dough into $1/4$-inch thick circle and place on top of filling. Cut remaining dough off with a knife and then pinch to seal edges. Cut some vent holes in the top of the pie. Cover and bake, using 8 coals underneath the oven and 17 on top, for 50 minutes or until top is golden brown and filling is bubbly.

Apple-Almond Mince Pie

10-inch Dutch oven
28 hot coals
8 servings

Crust

4¹/₄ cups flour
1 cup shortening
¹/₂ cup butter-flavored shortening
¹/₂ teaspoon salt
2 tablespoons sugar
1 cup hot water
1 egg, beaten
Coarse sugar

Filling

3 medium Granny Smith apples, cored, pared, and thinly
   sliced
4 tablespoons flour
3 tablespoons butter, melted
1 jar (27 ounces) mincemeat
¹/₂ cup slivered almonds, toasted and chopped
¹/₂ teaspoon almond extract

See page 10 for tips on removing pie from Dutch oven before starting the recipe.

To make the crust; using a large bowl, cut flour, shortenings, salt, and sugar with a pastry cutter until crumbs are all of equal size. Add water and gently toss with a fork just to moisten. Divide dough into two equal parts, and pat out first half to form a disk on a well-floured board. Roll dough to $1/4$-inch thickness. Place in a lightly greased Dutch oven to cover bottom and halfway up the sides.

For the filling; toss apples with flour and butter in a large bowl. In medium bowl, mix mincemeat with almonds and extract. Put apples in Dutch oven and cover with mincemeat mixture.

Pat and roll out remaining dough. Place top crust in place and seal edges with water. Cut vent holes in top crust, then brush with egg and sprinkle with coarse sugar. Cover and bake, using 8–10 coals underneath the oven and 16–18 on top, for 10–15 minutes. Then reduce heat by removing 4 coals from underneath the oven and 2 coals from the top. Bake 30–35 minutes or until golden brown.

Caramel-Pumpkin Cheesecake

(2) 10-inch Dutch ovens
6-inch Dutch oven
47 hot coals
8 servings

Crust

2^1/$_2$ cups graham cracker crumbs
^{3}/$_4$ cup finely chopped pecans
^{3}/$_4$ cup sugar
10 ^{1}/$_2$ tablespoons melted butter
^{3}/$_4$ teaspoon ginger
^{3}/$_4$ teaspoon cinnamon

Filling

3 packages (8 ounces each) cream cheese
^{3}/$_4$ cup brown sugar
^{1}/$_2$ cup granulated sugar
4 eggs
2^1/$_2$ tablespoons flour
1 teaspoon cinnamon
^{1}/$_2$ teaspoon nutmeg
^{1}/$_4$ teaspoon ground cloves
Pinch salt
1^1/$_2$ cups pumpkin

Caramel Sauce

1 cup and 2 tablespoons sugar
$2^1/2$ tablespoons water
$1/2$ teaspoon lemon juice
1 tablespoon Karo syrup
1 cup heavy cream
2 tablespoon butter
$1/2$ teaspoon vanilla

To make the crust; combine all of the crust ingredients in a medium bowl and spoon into 10-inch Dutch oven. Press crust mixture to cover bottom and $1^1/2$ inches up the sides of oven. Cover and bake, using 6 coals underneath the oven and 10 on top, for 5 minutes.

For the filling; beat cream cheese and sugars in a large bowl. Add eggs one at a time, mixing well with each addition. Combine dry ingredients in a small bowl and then add to the cream cheese mixture. Beat in pumpkin. Pour over crust, cover, and bake, using 6 coals underneath the oven and 10–11 on top, for 1 hour and 20 minutes. Cool 15 minutes, then refrigerate for 3 hours.

To prepare the sauce; bring sugar, water, and lemon juice to a boil in 10-inch Dutch oven over 8–10 coals. Add syrup and cook until golden amber color, approximately 20 minutes. Meanwhile, heat cream in 6-inch Dutch oven over 4 coals, but do not boil. Take syrup off heat and mix in cream. It will foam up, so be careful. Stir in butter and vanilla. Pour into a container and allow to cool. Use as a topping on individual servings.

Something-to-Crow-About Carrot Cake

(2) 12-inch Dutch ovens
48 hot coals
12 servings

Cake

(double for 2-layer cake)
1 cup oil
4 eggs
1$^1/_2$ cups brown sugar
1 teaspoon vanilla
1$^1/_2$ teaspoons rum extract
1 cup buttermilk
2 cups flour
$^1/_2$ teaspoon salt
$^1/_2$ teaspoon cinnamon
$^1/_2$ teaspoon nutmeg
$^1/_4$ teaspoon ground ginger
2 teaspoons baking soda
$^3/_4$ cup grated carrots
1 cup baby food carrots
1 cup shredded coconut

Frosting

(double for a 2-layer cake)
1 package (8 ounces) cream cheese
$^1/_2$ cup butter
2 teaspoons grated orange peel
1 teaspoon vanilla
2 cups powdered sugar

To make the cake; cream oil, eggs, and sugar in a large bowl. Then add vanilla, rum extract, and buttermilk; mixing completely. In a medium bowl, combine flour, salt, cinnamon, nutmeg, ginger, and baking soda; stir into the creamed mixture until well blended. Fold in carrots, baby food carrots, and coconut. Pour into greased Dutch oven with parchment circle in the bottom. Cover and bake, using 10 coals underneath the oven and 14 on top, for approximately 20 minutes or until toothpick in center comes out clean. Cool and flip out cake onto a 12-inch Dutch oven lid, take off parchment and let cool. Repeat process for second layer.

For the frosting; using a large bowl, combine cream cheese and butter together until well blended, add orange peel and vanilla. Mix in powdered sugar and stir until spreading consistency. Repeat process for second layer. Spread frosting on cooled cake and decorate.

The recipe is courtesy of Damon Faust.

Spicy Applesauce Cake with Caramel Icing

(2) 12-inch Dutch ovens
10-inch Dutch oven
34 hot coals
8–10 servings

Cake

2 cups flour
1 tablespoon unsweetened cocoa
1^1/2 cups sugar
1 teaspoon each ground cinnamon, nutmeg, allspice,
 and cloves
1^1/2 teaspoons baking soda
1 teaspoon salt
^{1}/2 cup shortening
2 cups applesauce
2 eggs, lightly beaten
^{1}/2 cup semisweet chocolate chips
^{1}/2 cup chopped walnuts
1 cup raisins

Topping

^{1}/2 cup semisweet chocolate chips
^{1}/2 cup chopped walnuts

Caramel Icing

$^1/_4$ cup brown sugar
4 tablespoons heavy cream or half-and-half
2 tablespoons butter
Pinch of salt
$^1/_2$ cup powdered sugar

To make the cake; in a large bowl, combine dry ingredients. Add shortening, applesauce, and eggs; beat until well mixed. Stir in chocolate chips, walnuts, and raisins and pour into greased 12-inch Dutch oven.

Combine topping ingredients and sprinkle over batter in Dutch oven. Cover and bake, using 10 coals underneath the oven and 14 coals on top, for 35–40 minutes or until cake tests done.

For the icing; place 2 cups water in 12-inch Dutch oven and bring to simmer over 10 coals. Place 10-inch Dutch oven in water. Heat brown sugar, cream, butter, and salt until sugar is dissolved. Cool to room temperature. Then beat in powdered sugar until smooth. Drizzle icing over cake.

Index

Metric Conversion Chart

Volume Measurements		Weight Measurements		Temperature Conversion	
U.S.	**Metric**	**U.S.**	**Metric**	**Fahrenheit**	**Celsius**
1 teaspoon	5 ml	$^1/_2$ ounce	15 g	250	120
1 tablespoon	15 ml	1 ounce	30 g	300	150
$^1/_4$ cup	60 ml	3 ounces	90 g	325	160
$^1/_3$ cup	75 ml	4 ounces	115 g	350	180
$^1/_2$ cup	125 ml	8 ounces	225 g	375	190
$^2/_3$ cup	150 ml	12 ounces	350 g	400	200
$^3/_4$ cup	175 ml	1 pound	450 g	425	220
1 cup	250 ml	$2^1/_4$ pounds	1 kg	450	230

TERRY LEWIS,

with the help of his daughter Tori, is a two-time winner of the World Championship Cook-offs held by the International Dutch Oven Society. He has been cooking and competing in Dutch oven events for over twenty years and occasionally uses his expertise to judge cooking competitions. Terry has four children and enjoys life on his farm outside of Tabiona, Utah.